Ancient Peoples of Africa From Egypt to the Great Zimbabwe Empire History for Kids

Children's Ancient History Books

Left Brain Kids

Educational Books for Children

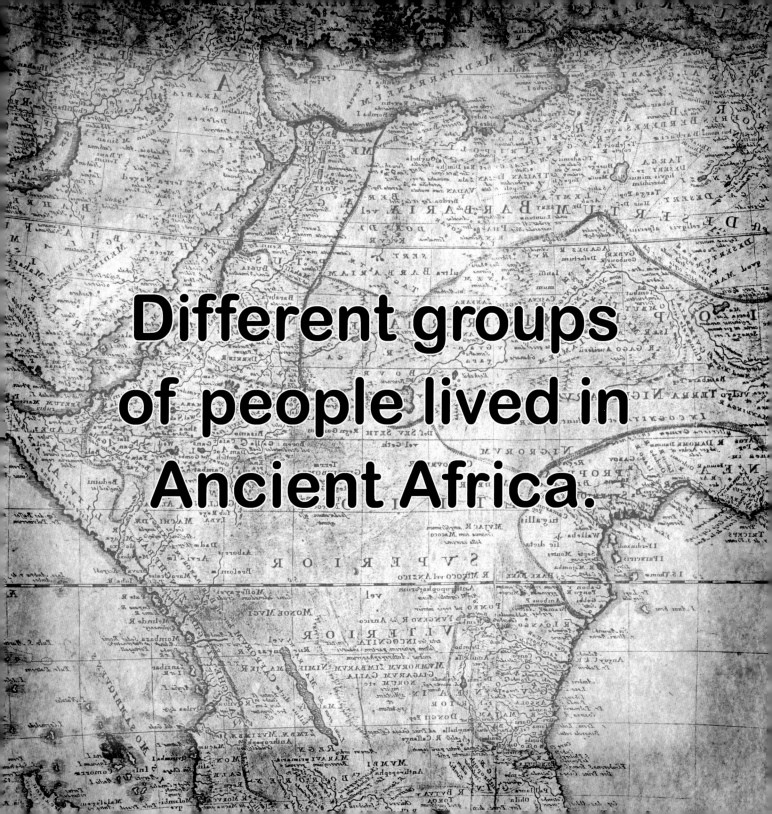

Different groups of people lived in Ancient Africa.

The first European colony, led by Dutchman Jan van Riebeek, was established in Cape Town, South Africa in 1653.

As this colony developed, people from the Netherlands, France, and Germany arrived. These people became called "Boers", which means "farmer".

In 1800, the British gained control of the land and this made the Boers unhappy.

The Boers then decided to leave and make a new colony in the north and east regions of South Africa.

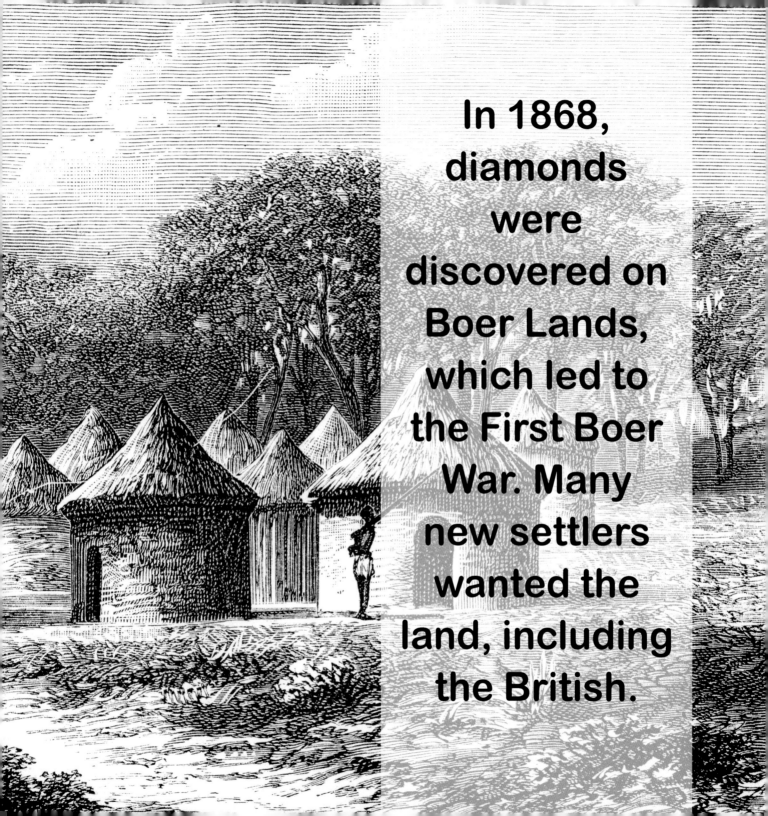

In 1868, diamonds were discovered on Boer Lands, which led to the First Boer War. Many new settlers wanted the land, including the British.

The Boers won the First Boer War against the British.

In 1886, gold was discovered on another part of Boer Land, which led to another war known as the Second Boer War.

This time, the British won and claimed the disputed Boer Lands.

After the Second Boer War, most Boers left South Africa and moved to Argentina, Kenya, Mexico, and the United States.

Meanwhile in Egypt, the Greek ruler, Alexander the Great, established the Ptolemy Dynasty.

One of the famous members of the Ptolemy Dynasty was Cleopatra, who claimed to be the reincarnation of the Egyptian god Isis.

When Cleopatra's father, Ptolemy VII died, she and her ten-year-old brother, Ptolemy VIII were married and ruled Egypt as co-rulers.

As Cleopatra's brother grew older he began to want more power and eventually forced Cleopatra away from the palace.

Cleopatra regained her power when she met with Roman ruler Julius Caesar, who helped her defeat his brother. Cleopatra's brother drowned in the Nile River.

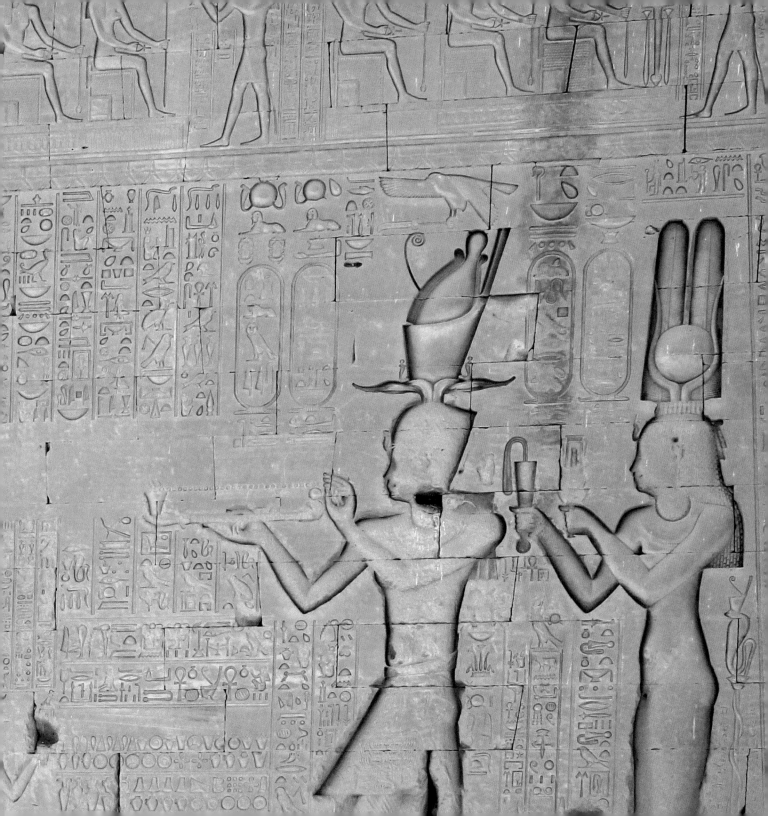

While in central Africa, the powerful city-state of Great Zimbabwe was formed. It was untouched by European colonizers, who only settled on coastal areas.

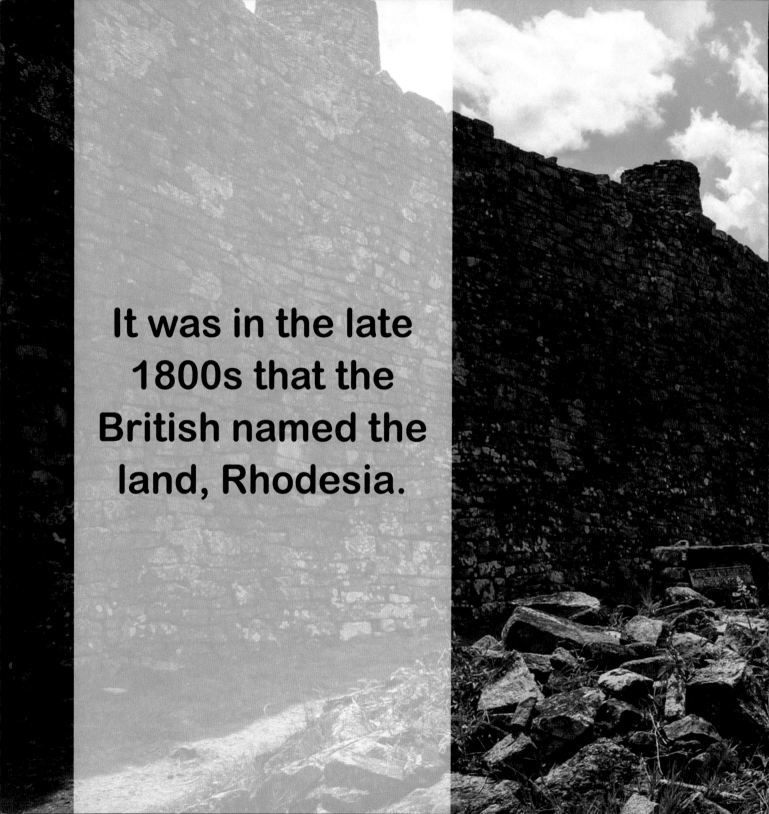

It was in the late 1800s that the British named the land, Rhodesia.

In 1923, the British divided Rhodesia: the Southern Rhodesia, which is now Zimbabwe and the Northern Rhodesia, which is now Zambia.

There is much more to know about Ancient African History. Research and have fun!

Made in the
USA
Monee, IL